AF584407

Wakefield Press

This Life in Rhymes and Riddles

Born and raised in Adelaide, Heather Caddick has had a diverse career spanning kindergarten teaching to stockbroking and investment. She has always been passionate about voluntary work, encompassing wildlife and humanitarian causes in Africa. When she is not travelling, she lives in Adelaide with her husband, Alfie.

Heather is the author of *For the Love of Rhinos (and this life)*, and *The Road Less Travelled (and being curious). This Life in Rhymes and Riddles* is her first book of poetry.

This Life in Rhymes and Riddles

Heather Caddick

Wakefield Press

Wakefield Press
16 Rose Street
Mile End
South Australia 5031
wakefieldpress.com.au

First published 2018

Edited by Julia Beaven, Wakefield Press
Designed by Liz Nicholson, designBITE
Typeset by Michael Deves, Wakefield Press

ISBN 978 1 74305 572 4

A catalogue record for this book is available from the National Library of Australia

Wakefield Press thanks Coriole Vineyards for continued support

For Tilda, Emmy and Natalia

Contents

War

Boer War

6th South Australian Imperial Bushmen, Trooper 538

Answering a call to war,
bushmen, rifles, steeds and more
would help the British fight the Boers,
Imperial Bushmen to the core,
with Queen and Crown to fund it all.

One in ten were pre-selected;
nine of ten would be rejected.
Bushmen, marksmen, horsemen too
meant city boys should miss the queue.

Douglas Eard, eighteen and on the farm,
that never did him any harm.
Bush life, cattle, horses, shearing,
were in his make up and his breeding.

The recruiters liked him: 'He's one of the best.
A natural horseman, up to the test.
Rank him Trooper, number 538
in Mounted Rifles, among his mates.'

Douglas Eard met those from near and far,
with Breaker Morant forever their star.
April the sixth, nineteen hundred and one,
Warrigul sails with all farewells done.

The seas are so calm, the days are so long
spent tending the horses and cleaning the stalls.
There's mateship and yarns, and obeying the calls
of officers, sporting their medals and braid
with stories of battles that had them afraid
but break up the boredom of everyday drill.
These yarns of their valour, just add to the thrill,
and spicing their stories, puts Troopers in awe
of forthcoming battles confronting the Boers.

Their docking, dispatch, marks a change in the war.
The Brits major victory has shattered the Boers.
Veldt charges means thousands of horsemen are dead –
the Boers have been vanquished, but re-group instead
as guerrillas, and still fighting hold fast to their cause.
British troops are disrupted, supply lines are blocked,
arms caches are raided, explosives are hocked.

The British commanders have few horsemen left
with true riding talent, and marksmen to boot.
They welcome the Aussies, with no training plan,
there's instant deployment, no time to adjust
to the change of environment, the heat and the dust.
Their haphazard mission, to form posse groups
as fighting guerrillas – no need for troops.

Farms must be plundered, removing the cattle,
plus horses and wagons, last used in the battle.
Round up the women and children and chattels
and march them like ants to concentration camps.
By far the best method to keep them away
from aiding their people by night and by day.
Small Boer encampments, destroy them at dawn,
Ride through the night, rest after the morn.

The Aussie Imperial Bushmen deployed
Trooper 538, just one of the boys.
His horse True Blue – steady, brave and strong –
will last the distance, eleven months long.
The vast veldt transected for 3000 K,
riding through night and sweating all day,
surviving the skirmishes, blocking his way.
Death of the horses, typhoid and despair,
bad water, dysentery laid them all bare.
Poor food and heat stroke, struck many down.
The final drum beats; a truce has been found.

The year is now nineteen hundred and two
and the 'Gentlemen's War' is finally through.
More died from illness than fighting the war,
the toll on the horses far bigger than all.
Harry 'The Breaker' Morant disobeyed
and a kangaroo court made sure that he paid.
While the others prepared to make their trip home
to family and loved ones, no longer to roam.

Travel, adventure, Imperial causes
brought shock, disillusionment, mental disorders.

Farewelling True Blue is a bittersweet test.
D.E. finds a family to take him to rest
on their farm near the veldt, where his valour impressed.

Aussie bush and the farm pulls Douglas Eard home.
The saddle, his token from fighting the Boers
at his side as he docks on Australian shores.
It takes pride of place, when he's back on the farm
and is central to telling the Great Boer War yarn.

DOUGLAS EARD GOLDSMITH, author's grandfather, 1882–1951

Second World War
Western Desert Campaign, Tobruk

2/43 Infantry,
Captain John Colman Hodgetts

A Pact of Steel joins the Tiber to Rhine
with the rise of Fascism in '39.
An Axis of power between Berlin and Rome
expanding all borders to claim as their own.

Civil chaos in Spain, the Bolshevik mess,
Karl Marx ideology brewing unrest.
Their answer is Fascism, and put to the test,
control all the problems besetting the West.

With war declared, the Allies assemble,
thoughts of another World War make them tremble.
With countries in Europe like dominoes falling,
Commonwealth countries now answer the calling,
sifting, enlisting, conscripting, deploying.

The theatre of war is now expanding,
Northern Africa, Egypt and Palestine
have treasures to annex, their positions are prime
for backing the military with force maritime,
replenishing troops and garrisons held,
taking care of the wounded, respecting those felled.

John, Ken and Joe were schoolboys together
at Adelaide's Collegiate School of St Peter.
Football and sports linked their teenage years,
Victor Harbor their choice with school holiday peers.
Family business expected for their careers.
All three gave their names, without delay,
growing excitement at going away.

Tobruk, a small port on the Libyan coast,
soon to become their Western Desert post.
The Aussie contingent must hold the blockade,
British ships at the port will supply them with aid.

Our boys adjust quickly, arriving in waves.
Build dugouts or shelter in hollows and caves.
Artillery action brings more tank attacks,
with booby traps, mines and low mortar flacks.
Hellish heat, blinding dust and stifling sand
does little to dull this merry band.

Mateship and laughter quell freezing cold nights,
Aussie larrikins show off, their spirits high
with humour and hijinks and joking and more
facing eight months of hell winning this war.
Unorthodox tactics, not seen in the book –
they're soon to be labelled 'The Rats of Tobruk'.

AMF's youngest captain, John Hodgetts by name,
is picking up wounded, the injured, the lame.
A small army truck, with an open-back tray
can deliver these soldiers away from the fray.
The driver will take them with just a short trip
to the port where there waits a hospital ship.

At the back of the truck, Captain John stands,
legs akimbo and gripping the sides with his hands.
The enemy aims, and a mortar shell lands
on the truck, that explodes in a blinding flash,
blasted to smithereens in just a dash.

Joe watches this happen and later, with Ken,
asks for permission to bring back the men.
Superior officers deny their request:
'We need you surviving, not dead with the rest!'
It's a charred maze of metal, with fire all around,
That takes these brave souls to a more hallowed ground.

Three mates are now two, but soon to be one,
With Ken killed in action, one week after John.

Rommel breaks the garrison, bringing defeat,
and the Allies are cornered, and start to retreat.
The Brits go to Egypt, the Aussies to Greece –
three more years of fighting, before there is peace.

JOHN COLMAN HODGETTS, author's uncle, killed in action 17.7.42.

KENNETH CHARLES BARRITT killed in action 28.7.42.

JOSEPH WILLCOX CARLISLE STEVENS, survived Tobruk and related this story to the author in 2016, aged 97.

Second World War
Middle East and Kokoda Trail

2/16 Infantry,
Captain Douglas Keith Goldsmith

Tales of privation of daring and more
were told round our table, to settle the score.
A way to trim sails, with rules for us four.
Keith's childhood, a benchmark shown off as a dampening
for these times of peace, of ease and of pampering.

Grandparents and relatives, scarred by the war,
embraced this new era, their mourning now done
by living new lives, through the lives of their young.

Keith's tales of his childhood and farm life in Northam,
embellished with exploits, black snakes and wild horses,
strict parents, six children, a lasting impression
of struggling and working to beat the Depression.

School three miles down a well-trodden track
reached with two kids astride horse's back.
Keith and the eldest would walk close behind,
then tether their nag, tie a nosebag of chaff,
and enter the school with a whoop and a laugh.

The classroom was filled with varying ages –
one teacher adjusting curriculum stages.

Life in the country town widened to Perth –
sports, education, community work.
Freedom still curbed by economy's woes,
farm work, resilience to nature's extremes,
meant curbing the longing to realise his dreams.

Turmoil in Europe is gathering pace;
Spain's Civil War and Nazism's face.
'Germany over all', the little man states
in speeches galore, with parades and marches
enlisting the youth, creating codes of behaviour,
creeds and songs adoring their Führer.

The countries of Europe, like dominoes fall
with England at risk to the fate of them all.
War is declared with a call to arms
that has Aussies conscripted from cities and farms.

With adventure beckoning, Keith volunteers.
Joins leadership training, is schooled with his peers,
and is made a captain of infantry troops –
his father admiring his shiny new boots.

The diggers set sail, with Cairo their base
and glorious weeks of waiting take place,
augmented by nurses, now housed on the Nile
with parties and romance, jasmine, gardenias,
colonial clubs with manicured lawns,
jazz groups and cabaret, playing till dawn.
A slice of paradise away from the front
awaiting their orders from High Command;
with instructions deploying new battleground.

It's a march to Palestine, held by the Vichy,
with an Allied attack, backed by the Navy,
to occupy Lebanon and take Beirut
ensuring a block to German advances
and protecting the Suez, they can't take chances.

They manage to cross the Litani River
under fire from the Vichy, they try to deliver
support that is needed on lateral flanks,
then move further north, uniting their ranks.
Tank bombardment leads to casualties galore –
their first real encounter with battlefront war.

Our men form groups with guerrilla-style strategy
overwhelming the enemy with persistence and gallantry.
Through lush orange orchards and small grassy fields,
ditches and gullies provide safety when there's a need
to tend to the wounded and plan their next lead.

Two-sixty-nine fallen, two-seventy left,
Four weeks of fighting, Vichy French bereft.
A truce is signed, and the conquest is noted
with a march through Beirut, their people elated.
The diggers now peacekeepers, with time out to rest
before the next order at HC's behest.

December '41, Japan enters the war.
The prime minister orders a swift troop recall.
Pearl Harbor prompts action, and our Douglas Keith
sets sail for Fremantle with the 2nd/16th.

The Japanese land on New Guinea's north coast,
ten thousand strong, and their strategy boast
is to march to Port Moresby, across the long rise,
jungle tracks and mountains will lead to the prize.
Large airfields and Australia just over the water –
this Empire expansion would rival Herr Hitler.

Within days, the men from 2nd/16th
are rushed to New Guinea, the plan is to thwart
the advancement of Japanese troops from the north.
They'll climb ridges and peaks of the jungle track,
confront and disperse all dugout positions,
disrupting supplies of their stores and munitions.

D. Keith is captain to an able platoon
that starts its long trek just after noon.
Jungle paths are enclosed by tunnels and foliage,

mossy roots to slip on, mist, mud and deluge.
No sunlight and leeches that cling to your socks,
bully beef and biscuit supplies in a box.

Fighting begins with Japanese snipers
emerging from dugouts to pick out their targets.
The nights are alive with taunting and echoes,
Japanese yell through megaphones, sending a warning:
'We shall find and kill you all in the morning.'

Food rations are scant, there's rotten rice licked
from banana leaves, and those bland soggy bics.
Malaria, dysentery, damp and cold nights
means sleeping evades them, but not mozzie bites.
Fuzzy Wuzzy bearers never complain,
they make stretchers from blankets to hammock the maimed.
These heroes persist with the ultimate boast
not one living casualty is left at his post.

By evading, retreating and counter attack,
these 'Ragged Bloody Heroes' defend the track.
Horii's forces are stranded on the final ridge
overlooking Port Moresby, they're vanquished and beat.
Japanese High Command calls a retreat.

This valiant fight from tree to tree
sees the Aussie flag flying on November three,
1942 the year. There's six hundred dead
and a thousand men wounded, broken and bleeding.

Douglas Keith moves to Adelaide, now a family man,
the flame-haired Diana has taken his hand.
And four children later, the stories we heard
were of his childhood in Northam, of sports and of fun –
those grim tales of wartime were never spun.

DOUGLAS KEITH GOLDSMITH, author's father, 1918–1995

D.K. Goldsmith interviewed by Peter Brune in May 1987.
Those Ragged Bloody Heroes by Peter Brune, published by Allen and Unwin, 1991.

Growing Up

Childhood

1950s, Adelaide

Stannington Avenue, near to the park,
creeks gurgled in winter, trees shaded, dogs barked.
Young families nurtured in houses with yards
and no fences, just lawns, and with wide open doors
for neighbours to borrow and lend for their chores
a mower, some sugar, an egg or a trailer –
community life without fear or favour.

The baker delivered, the milkman as well,
children ran free, and would strongly rebel
against fuss and control, but exceptional coddling,
was allowed from their grandparents, doting and hovering.

The park was our mecca for freedom and fun,
to dam up the creeks and watch waters run,
catch tadpoles, make cubbies, play hidey and rest
in hollows of tree trunks, watch birds in their nests.

The ship's bell rang loudly from over the road,
our mother's best method to summon her herd.
Its toll proclaimed dinner was ready to serve,
shepherd's pie, rhubarb, custard and, make no mistake,
we scampered back home, the dog in our wake.
This kelpie we heard later was in deep disgrace,

dead neighbourhood chooks sealing his fate,
made worse because one of us opened the gate.
A friendly farmer took Yogi away
to round up his sheep, so now work would be play.

With four kids our house will burst at the seams,
but down the road there's a bigger one, fulfilling our dreams.
Large gardens surrounded by hedges, gum trees,
a Moreton Bay fig, plum trees covered in bees.
There are citrus too, vegetables, corn on the cob –
and plenty of space for a fast-growing mob.

A millstone forever, the neighbours gossip and chatter,
to buy such a mansion – but what does that matter?
The decision is made, the documents signed,
we children unpack, our parents unwind.

Slowly and surely we settle down here
with working bees, sleepovers, barbies with beer.
Mario from Italy lives in the annex, completely alone,
his Calabrian sweetheart waiting at home
for a life to be forged on this new stable ground,
she'll then travel to marry him, Adelaide bound.

He adopts his new home with our family in spades
takes charge of the garden, a jack of all trades.
Finds work with a car maker, no job is too great,
And soon he is Father's dear friend, his best mate.

A tennis court, drawn out and measured with string,
is levelled and planted and ready by spring.
Treehouses are built in the Moreton Bay fig
only tops of trees visible, above them the clouds.
We call the house 'Treetops', and the name is allowed.

A clique of children from houses around
Meet in our cellar, deep in the ground,
a secret kids' clubhouse where passwords gain entry,
the youngest must stand by the steps as a sentry.
Our exploits are planned, just after dark,
to creep after strangers in Tusmore Park
recording their movements with paper and pen,
and regrouping at the clubhouse just after ten.

A gruff schoolteacher who lives nearby
needs a fright, we decide, so we plan to tie
a long piece of string round the knob of her door,
pull it gently, and watch her open it scowling
to no one! Our laughter soon turns into howling.
Rollerskating the streets makes cars slow to stalling,
they wave and encourage our behaviour appalling.
This freedom makes daring to skate even faster,
Grant Avenue central, the best one to master.

Summer heat means beach days spent at Moana,
cars parked on the sand with shade from cabanas
and umbrellas, card tables and eskies unloaded,
steamer chairs, surf and skim boards de roaded.

Zinc on the nose, and floppy beach hats,
no parents control us, all children can swim,
and surfing is mastered with practice and whim
by letting the body surf in on a wave.
A dumping in turbulent seas makes us brave.
Racing on surfboards, so far to the shore,
paddling back out again, keen to catch more.

The adult world fascinates, old friends and neighbours,
we spy and discuss their different behaviours.
The drawing room laden with bowers of flowers,
glamour dressing has obviously taken them hours.
The tipsy, the scary, the wary, the smoker –
we give each a nickname, but behaving our best,
angelically offer the nibbles to guests.

There's one surly neighbour we plan to take to task,
fill a scotch egg with mustard, and offer him last.
He gasps, and chokes, but aims for decorum,
gives thrill to our prank, but our mother's in trauma.

Sports and squabbles where friends become foes,
and foes become friends again, and so it goes
in this childhood mix of freedom and fun
with a place in the group for everyone.
Families together, kids happy and healthy,
But Australia becoming a land of the wealthy.
The decade of hope, a phrase for the fifties,
Soon to become a maze in the sixties.

A Teenager's Life

1960s, Adelaide

Schooldays are bound in rules and convention,
my girls-only college has tradition, pretension,
with manners, decorum and dress codes to hone
this school prides itself as a male-free zone.
Assemblies with march-ins, sermons and hymns,
with reporting of pupil transgressions and sins –
like girls who talk and lag on street corners,
gloveless or hatless, beyond the school gate,
a monitor squeals and determines your fate.
Engulfed by religion, the Bible's lessons
are used for punishment, in weekly detention.

Education comes second to morals for daughters.
Schooling must steer us through life's turbulent waters.
'Boys are the problem!' – we exchange knowing glances,
determined to meet more and take our chances.
'No grouping or chatting or meeting in delis
for milkshakes and sodas, or playing transistors!
Steer clear of Norwood, where bodgies and widgies
display such appalling licentious behaviour,
Wear stovepipes and leathers, and show off regalia.

Skirt lengths are ruled, and measured whilst kneeling –
whatever you do, don't look at the ceiling.
For a cool mini skirt bend forward, don't stress,
and the length of the skirt becomes two inches less.

Our school is renowned for its strict moral code
with one social milestone, a road to be trod.
Kings College and Saints boys all vie for the chance
of a prized invitation to our formal school dance.
Fifth and sixth formers attend this school ball
where teachers are seated around the dance hall
and parents will form a human chain link
to direct us to supper, so there's never a chance
to savour the moonlight and delights of romance.

The stairs are blockaded with wire intertwined,
all potential for decadent trysts now sidelined.
Then comes the dress code of modest decorum –
no minis, low necklines, nor peroxided hair,
string straps on a bodice, nor backbones laid bare.

You may think these rules made us shudder in shame
but quite the reverse, we were atop of their game.
This infamous formal, the best in our town,
fun, laughter and mischief, a night of renown.
The last dance is over, we pile into cars
and head for the hills, to study the stars.

The Melbourne Cup race in November is fun.
We sixth formers plan a sweep to be won.
The bets are collected,
the horses allotted,
a transistor handy, and just before three,
I make an excuse to go out for a wee.
The race is exciting, I write down the winners,
a nice little dividend paid to the grinners.
But, sadly, a swot with a nasty conjecture
reports to our teacher this sinful adventure.

We're marched to the headmistress, assemble a forum,
she's frazzled and frayed by our lack of decorum.
We're admonished and cautioned, with lectures, advice,
and sworn to silence, with vows to reform and be nice.

In balance, this school of censure and propriety
has tempered the gulf between home and security.
Rigid rules prompt questions, while keeping alert
to adult behaviour and beliefs they assert.
I'd say it strengthened the will to persist
and aim for the goals they threatened with risk.
The era of teenage rebellion is here,
old modes of behaviour will soon disappear.

Now aged sixteen, the chains are unleashed
with the licence to drive the goal to be reached.
Show a certified birth, pay over the counter,
climb into the seat, parents adjacent.

Slip the gear stick to first, hear instructions and yakking
with road rules and tips from my parents as backing.
Three brothers full of envy, their sister now driving
a pre-owned Ford Prefect, and she can't stop smiling.

Our family weekender for skiing and fun
sits plumb on the river. A fifty-mile run
through winding hills on roads with challenging corners –
Devil's Elbow is famous for turning manoeuvres.
There's danger in speed, but such freedom to roam
and the gods must have smiled and left me alone
(the fastest time clocked, fifty minutes to home).

Forbidden to travel without a degree
I decide that it's pre-school teaching for me.
Three years as a student, to qualify fully,
I think of my father as some kind of bully.
But comply with his orders, my aim is to travel,
see the world, face the music that constantly plays
like Hamlin's Pied Piper, to take me away.

The teaching college, a cloistered arena,
strict rules, expectations and codes of behaviour.
Quaint maiden-aunt lecturers, with victims and pets,
a male-free zone, with one exception –
There's a master for art in his nest of deception.
Louche and suave, dark-haired and brooding,
A perfect foil to teenage schmoozing.

One delightful spark of human reality,
the brilliant and humorous head of psychology.
Lectures with passion, satire and fun,
she breaks the tedium and shines a bright light
on life's possibilities, like day after night.

Parties and dance dates appear in my diary
with private debutante balls for variety.
Tennis courts marqueed, and brimming with flowers,
dance floors and live bands for dancing the hours.
Programs are issued, each dance needs a tick,
with a partner allotted, you hope to be picked.
If a dance has no booking, you glide to the loo
and wait for the next dance, and partner anew.
Steady boyfriends tick the last dance as their own,
with the added enticement of escorting you home.

Three years of study with new friends and old
sees a budding awareness of our world unfold –
Vietnam, Bay of Pigs, a man on the moon,
democracy, Fascism, Cold War and Communism,
tertiary activism, Adelaide conservatism.

This world's vast variety of complex confusion,
good among bad, beauties and beasts,
wonders and spectacles outside our land,
prompt a compulsion in me to see it firsthand –
with my mother's hopes dashed for that gold wedding band.
The deal has been sealed, graduation is done,
and the travel road beckons like a rising sun.

Grown-up

Marriage and Careers

1970s, Adelaide - Melbourne - Adelaide

Mum's dreams of a wedding are realised at last
with a date for the nuptials; the long wait is past.
To be single in Adelaide, well into your twenties,
no husband to speak of, your life must be empty.
The groom to be is not Adelaide bred,
at least not a Catholic! The daughter will wed
a Kenyan-born Englishman, relief at her choice,
a white Anglo Saxon, a bond to rejoice.

The wedding is planned with strategic precision:
a reception, dancing and dinner the decision.
On the tennis court sits a marquee of flowers,
family and friends have been working for hours
with chatter and laughter, excitement is building,
the countdown begins and the pressure's unyielding.
Twelve tables for ten are place-named with care,
the great-aunts will be a problem to bear.
Both deaf, with loud voices they shout when they speak,
with mauve hair and fur capes, they'll frighten the meek.

The big day is here, and three months of drought
is broken by rainfall, a deluge no doubt.
The service conducted 'To love, not obey',
umbrellas to dinner as dance bands play.

The atmosphere dazzling to young and to old,
the great-aunts are booming, part of the fold.
The garden is lit, spotlighting the trees,
loved grandfather joking, a child on his knees.
The rain pitter-patters on the marquee awning,
and the dancing continues until early morning.
The speeches are over, followed by toasts,
And the new married couple escapes to the coast.

The seventies decade stirs the young to rebel,
to question old codes of expected behaviour,
life paths and politics, the status of women.
Male-dominant workplaces open their doors
to women offloading their household chores.
Independence to work is made easier by far
with motherhood paused, the pill is a star.
Networks for women with flair and verve
spur confidence and change in an upward curve.
I am woman, hear me roar the pop star sings,
we shall open the door without apron strings.
The message is strong and helps to create
a new gender balance. Time for female rebate.

We settle in Melbourne, the husband and I,
two careers in Collins Street, working close by.
I trade commodities, a dealer of sorts,
copper prices are rising and OPEC's a rort.
Placing orders for futures, a complex range
in Chicago, New York, London Metals Exchange.

The husband deals shares on the Stock Exchange floor
but our economy's slowing and trading is poor.
The Exchange is predicting an end to the boom,
recession is looming, the brokers in gloom.
A DCM ends two hundred careers –
'Don't come Monday' the order, employees in tears.
Surviving the turmoil is the focus for us,
a new job is seized, allaying the fuss.
By persistence – and with luck in the mix –
we continue our work lives, emerge from this fix.

Vietnam protests, the war worries Canberra,
our Diggers return with no pomp or regalia,
as if their brave service is shrouded in shame,
shoved under the carpet to shelve all the blame.
American coattails held tight till the last,
bringing decades of misery to those taking part.

We now have a basset hound, Karli by name.
Among Greeks in Prahran sits our house in a lane.
Side fences with neighbours topped up with glass,
broken shards sit in spikes no burglar can pass.
Strong friendships and bonds over ouzo are made,
happy times at the markets, their veggies displayed.

A new domesticity comes with the news
We're expecting a baby, careers need review.
We decide to be frugal, my work's put on hold:
one income, home duties, a new path unfolds.

It's junk shops and gardening, painting and sewing,
with friends and neighbours, home cooking is cursory,
wallpaper and paint make the office a nursery.

A February baby transforms our lives.
A dream child to care for, he sleeps like a lamb
with basset hound Karli curled under his pram.
Grandparents aren't here to hover, advise,
there's a gap and a yearning for strong family ties.
It's bitter winter, and with kero heaters, briquette fires
we try to heat our cold house. Night trips to the loo
mean donning a coat and ugg boots too.
Condensation forms on glass every morning
and I'm finding the endless routine rather boring.
The recession grinds on and we reach a forked road –
and return to Adelaide, easing the load.

The husband has laboured throughout the recession,
takes an offer, goes back to his former profession.
Nine months in Adelaide sees many changes,
an old house to work on, and new to the manger
is son number two, this one no dream baby.
Much loved by us all, despite lack of sleep,
a family of four is our quota to keep.

Late seventies panic in oil markets began
when revolution deposed the Shah of Iran.
The oil price doubled and economic troubles
saw gold becoming the only safe haven

for money world-wide, and OPEC is craven.
I accept an offer to deal in gold futures
and a casino of gambling takes over with gold.
A newspaper states: 'With this upward trend,
a gold ounce will purchase a Mercedes Benz.'

Excitement, elation and punters so bold,
gold fever goes viral for young and for old.
They invest in bullion if not futures they trade,
with the market price rising each trading day.
A bubble is forming, but punters don't question
the warning of losses, I dare to mention.
The phone rings with orders from dawn until dusk.
It's a circus with players spurred on by it all,
seemingly not caring that markets will fall.

The home front is eased with outside help.
A girl from the country spends weekdays with us
and cares for the boys without any fuss.
Then goes home on weekends, leaving us free
to spend time with each other, just the family.
We all steam along as the eighties approaches,
unaware of the turmoil that soon will encroach us.
The heady euphoria of gold-boom days,
the jokes and laughter about to change in a flash
when the market reverses and falls in a crash.

Optimism and Expanding Horizons

1980s, Adelaide

The new decade dawns in positive mode,
the trading desk busy, gold prices upload.
But a bubble is forming, the crisis is dire,
oil prices, inflation add fuel to the fire.
Then the Russians invade Afghanistan –
there's too much heat in this frying pan.
All bubbles must burst, gold halves in price,
and the galloping market slows down in a trice.

More losers than winners, a multiplication
that thrives on the drama of speculation.
Excitement and energy, punters take risks,
it's gold or real estate, shares or antiques –
they'll move on to the next in a couple of weeks.

Household chores and demands at work,
flexible hours, but it's hard not to shirk
two sons, two dogs and house disrepair.
My piano calms nerves of fatigue and despair
at not repeating my mother's domestic perfection.
Her daughter moves in a different direction,
acquiring diverse skills in her professional life –

a broker, a colleague, a working wife.
Foreign to all she was taught, but long overdue,
some women want work *and* careers to pursue.

We all get together for family weekends
stripping wallpaper, painting and making amends.
Grandparents, dogs and neighbours join too,
the shrieks and barks make it sound like a zoo.
Ropes loop hefty branches and glory vine creepers,
a wooden plank's fitted and tied down with care,
the new swing is ready to fly through the air.
A burn-off and barbecue roar into flame
with sausages sizzling and stuffed into rolls,
we crouch round the fire watching embers and coals.
The children climb hedges and play hide and seek
and this is our pattern to end every week.

Gorbachev, *glasnost*, the world seems more sane,
The curtain is lifting. They shout out his name:
'Gorby, Gorby!' and the door is ajar.
The Russian leader – prime minister, pop star?
He's quelling the threat, the Communist fear,
promising restructure, *perestroika* is here.
Such news seems strange heard from afar
with Communist doctrine a concept too far.

Houseboat adventures enter our lives,
my father's new passion, now he's retired.
It's a twelve-berth barge, square and large,
but easy to pilot, except into a wind.
It's moored on the Murray, near Tailem Bend.
The top deck is railed to spacious proportion,
the bridge downstairs, where he steers without caution.

The river bends and twists with islands and spits,
main flow to inlets and billabong outlets.
Grassy banks, small coves for campfires at night,
damper and marshmallow in ghostly moonlight.
There's birdsong till dusk, parrots that shriek,
the slow glide of pelicans watching us eat.
We read poems from Banjo, sing crude Aussie songs
of sheilas and jumbucks and swagmen forlorn.
The boys sink some yabbie pots and, if true to form,
they'll fill up with yabbies, well before dawn.

With children asleep we study the stars,
the Southern Cross dominates Venus and Mars.
A breeze stirs up ripples that sparkle and play –
these Riverland stories remain to this day.

A new era of women in broad shoulder pads,
power suits and high heels, the latest fads.
Business and commerce is noting their zeal,
law and medicine see the appeal.
The door opens wide in response to the challenge,

some reluctant, while others accept social change.
Women of merit with honours bestowed.
Media interest, networks and forums
give voice to the movement across the nation,
sardonically labelled 'emancipation'.

June '89 in Tiananmen Square,
students and workers in Beijing amass,
armed only with courage and veritas,
to rally for change, for freedom of speech,
but democratic China is way out of reach.
Government troops move in with their tanks
and massacre many, wound thousands more,
arrest and convict those remaining defiant,
organise trials before execution –
hunger strikes by the vanquished a solution.

But ripples travel, and like China's test,
East Europe is suffering civil unrest.
The Iron Curtain starts to shake and tremble,
more people protest, more people assemble.
Cold War ideology is crumbling and the Wall of Berlin,
built to divide and keep people in.
Armed soldiers at checkpoints shoot on sight
refugees climbing the Wall by day and by night.
The tremors get louder and trigger a reaction.
Authorities say, 'East Berliners are free
to cross through the borders, the West to see.'

Thousands queue, but jackhammers and picks
strike down the wall in less than a week.
Rejoicing and singing, 'Dark days are behind us
We're Germans together no creed will divide us.'

A ten-day trek in Nepal is a Christmas surprise
for our growing boys, to open their eyes.
Lead by Sherpas, we join a small group of campers,
tents, swags, basic food – no chance to be pampered.
We climb steep mountain paths, see breathtaking scenery,
with snow peaks above the neat terraced greenery.

A blizzard approaches with icy cold blasts,
we take refuge with villagers while the storm lasts.
Play cards, sing songs, cook yams and drink beer,
the Nepalese inn shakes with loud Christmas cheer.
Dawn brings the sun and the clearest of skies
as we embrace them and say our goodbyes.

Turbulence and Humanity

1990s

The economy's fading, the Stock Exchange fraught,
with recession, redundancies coming to naught.
The nineties begin with some trepidation,
oil market cartels by Middle East nations.
Iraq is the powerhouse, the leader Saddam
calls all the shots, America be damned!
Opposition grows and becomes an uproar,
as President Bush declares the Gulf War.

It's '91, and I'm spending time in Oman,
nestling the coastline, sublime Khorfakkan.
White sands and green sea, a stark mountain range,
a backdrop of shadows with red colours strange.
The coast curves and waves to the Straits of Hormuz,
the Persian Gulf and oil traffic's main route.

Lazily reading in beach-brolly shade,
waves gently lapping, I look out to sea
with shock and surprise, it's the US Navy
assembling in line across the horizon,
no sound but the menace of strength just beside us.
Warships and frigates, an aircraft carrier
protecting the Gulf for safe passage, no barrier.

The worldwide web is news to our boys.
Pacman and video games are their toys.
This internet marvel has made the world smaller,
and faster, and brighter, with Australia a follower.
Education agendas need to change gear,
IT knowledge now a must, to start a career.

The Cold War has finally run its full course,
the Soviet Union dissolves from its bourse.
New countries emerge from the shackles of power,
forming their governments, pulling down towers
of the Communist pyramid of state-owned assets:
'Sell them, own property, let enterprise rule!'
This scramble for change breeds all sorts of thuggery,
an unscrupulous race with no moral recovery.

Bill Clinton is president, America rules.
He tries to resolve the Middle East blues.
Diplomacy summits, the pendulum swings,
Palestine, Jewry, and there in the wings
are oil-rich Arabs, and Saddam the star,
Iran and Gulf States, oil flaunts its power.

The '90s saw growing awareness to environment ills,
the forests being cleared, the oceans are filled
with plastic and trash, coal fire belches fumes.
Overfed Western world, over-fished seas,
the slaughter of whales sends a message to heed
of the pace of destruction, the foul air we breathe.

Wildlife with no habitat, the balance is wrong.
We must redress this disaster, before it's all gone.

So Greenpeace assembles to fight for the whales,
environment lobbies plead, 'Get back on the rails,
Save the planet!' Carbon credits are born.
Trees for Life, let's recycle, becoming the norm.
It's a fight for survival, but the battle is tense
between profits and power, before change and good sense.

Eddie Mabo is fighting to change the law,
Aborigines could not own Country before.
He persuades the court, native title his aim,
the High Court decision supports his claim.
Today he is lauded, they call out his name.
Connection to Country, unique to their culture,
Songlines and Dreamtime, an ethnic right.
We swept their traditions way out of sight.
Cave paintings, message sticks, rites and knowledge,
where decisions were made by an Elder's college.
Survival and stories, related by chants,
celestial location, animals, plants.
An ancient culture deserves recognition,
and all should respect our Aboriginal tradition.

I'm in a small group, Ethiopia bound,
to monitor UNICEF projects on the ground.
Reporting on their progress rebuilding from famine,
new schooling for children, and primary care,

health for the mothers and the babies they bear.
Wars and unrest caused this famine extreme,
power in Addis was the Tigray rebels dream.

After landmines and mortars, schools are now rubble,
so they set up new classrooms away from the trouble
in calm woodland glades, whiteboards on a mound,
classes of ninety sit still on the ground,
one teacher, the children not making a sound.
Water wells sunk, means clean water, less illness,
women walk miles, carry pitchers and fill them.
Vaccination centres make children avoid
polio, cholera and deadly typhoid.
We fly back to Addis and note with dismay,
a plane wreck still visible near the runway.
Customs, security, a full-body search,
TV cameras and interviews note our research.

En route home via Eritrea,
Asmara lies in Italianate splendour.
Neat streets are bright with bougainvillea,
arched courtyard gardens beautify
the crumbling buildings of days gone by.
Pride in poverty, a stunning hive
of beautiful people, who fight to survive.

Fred Hollows name is famous here,
his cataract blindness work revered.
Blind people now see, and thanks to his fame
a new generation of boys bear his name.
Eritrea's a centre for ocular lenses,
a factory funded by donors and friends is
exporting the lenses, and restoring sight
for cataract blindness, yesterday's blight.
For Third World countries near and far,
Fred's lasting legacy is a shining star.

My ten years with UNICEF comes to completion.
Climate change, wildlife, threats of extinction
present a new focus well out of my range,
the Millennium looms and it's time for a change.

The Millennium

Wildlife and Habitats

Monarto Zoo, South Australia – Kruger Reserve, South Africa

The Millennium promises new things to some,
there's the Sydney Olympics and gold medals won.
Australia is riding the crest of a wave,
Iconic sports heroes, new footsteps to pave.
The euphoria spurs me to find something new –
I'll become a tour guide at an open-range zoo,
at Monarto, in the Mallee, just over the Hills.
Wild animals, nature, oh what a thrill
to indulge in my passion for all things wild –
urban life by comparison seems so mild.

There are lion, giraffe, rhinoceros too,
emu, ostrich and kangaroo,
with bison, oryx, meerkats and chimps,
zebra, hyenas and you might catch a glimpse
of cheetah or sable on your merry ride,
with commentary from a Monarto Zoo guide.

The course is intense. There's bio-diversity, botanical terms
history of taxons and behaviour to learn,
native species and habitats, I practice oration
and study at night in trepidation,
but manage to pass and soon wear with pride
the uniform of a Monarto Zoo guide.

Being with the animals one day a week
is a new world unfolding – more knowledge to seek.
Walking trails weave their way through the Park,
teachers and children think it's a lark
when a red kangaroo stops and stares,
of danger and fear she lives unaware.
Her pouch is bulging, a joey peeps out.
He's so large! It's probably time he jumped out.

Leroy and Levi are lion brothers true,
sit on the same mound, won't try somewhere new.
It's their vantage point under an island of trees,
elevated to catch an elusive breeze.
People in buses are staring as they pass by,
their cameras flashing at lions as they lie
both stretching and yawning, they look so bored,
their excited admirers are blankly ignored.

Uhura, the rhino, now has a calf.
The bomas constructed by vollies and staff,
with community help also in the mix
taking months to build fences, security fixed.

We can house many rhinos and answer the plea
for seven rhinos from Kruger to quarantine.
Monarto's the choice and is suited the best
as home for the rhinos, we pass all the tests!
A jumbo jet transfers them, Adelaide bound,
they travel with ease and seem happy aground.

Each individual has quite different traits:
curious, gentle, with feisty intelligence.
Satara, the alpha, is jealous and furious
Ibutho's a rival, and Uhura is curious.
His manhood is challenged, his status in doubt,
he barges the bomas with strength and breaks out.
Vets and zookeepers spend most of the day
trying to track him. Outpacing the fray,
he charges enclosures, security fencing,
is darted, keeps running despite this redressing.
By five o'clock weary and hungry, he turns –
time now for dinner, to his boma he returns.

A meerkat sentry is scanning the skies,
his duty to warn if a predator flies.
He might spot a wedgie, whose nest is nearby.
This Aussie eagle with wingspan enormous
swoops rabbits near burrows, clasps one with his claws,
flies over the meerkats, entrails in his jaws.
The sentry now peeps a shrill meerkat alarm –
and his family scampers to holes underground.

A six-week research camp in Kruger is booked,
with a leave pass granted from family, I'm hooked
to monitor wildlife, keep records and stats,
projects and programs in depth ethology
conducted by Pretoria University.

Camp base is deep in the African bush,
the Drakensberg Mountains away to the west.
Dense bushland and gorges sees Kruger at best.
A small house, two dormitories, doors open wide
to catch breezes, escaping the sheer heat outside.
A rondavel is kitchen, ablution block scant,
we are sixteen in total, all ages, post grads.
Americans and English, South Africans too,
we're excited to be in this open-range zoo.

Our focus, to study hyenas they've found,
a family whose den is a large termite mound.
They scavenge at night and sleep by the day,
look after their clan, scare predators away.

Our vigilance stops with dramatic force –
a young bull elephant changed his course,
rampaged through a village, from behind a tree
an African shot him with a 303.
This beautiful male is mortally wounded,
our ranger pursues and mercifully kills him.

Stricken and shocked, he returns ashen faced,
sits alone in silence, I see him weep,
this kind of killing is not part of his brief.

We camp one night, remote in the bush,
sleeping bags surround the fire,
jungle noises from the mire.
The crackle of twigs, the rustle of leaves,
an owl hoots and calls from the trees.
Lions roar, we hope they're far away,
but they roam all night and sleep by day.

Three-hour watch shifts are allotted –
midnight till three a.m. slotted.
Baboons are barking and grunting nearby,
they suddenly stop with one last cry.
It seems that the jungle is going to sleep,
the moon casts its spell and now I'm on guard,
spending my watch nervously playing cards.

This camp and Monarto over these past years,
have altered my life with new goals and new peers,
more like-minded people who work hard to share
our magical planet, the world must beware,
and change destructive behaviour, use political power
to save wildlife and habitats, humanity's bower.

The Great Australian Cattle Drive

2005, Birdsville

There is movement at the airport as the sun begins to rise,
Sleepy voices mask excitement as we take off for the skies.
The ground below is ochre red, the sky above is blue
when down we sweep to Birdsville to meet the cattle crew.
We taxi to the pub, blue heelers bark and run,
the locals slouch with beers in hand, hats angled against the sun.
They talk about the weather – 'No rain for months you know.
It's been as bad as '86, and God knows that was low.'

The Cattle Drive will travel from Birdsville to Maree,
five hundred head of cattle, drovers, stockmen riding free.
This track has rescued cattle for a hundred years or more,
dodging drought and finding feed, the drovers know it all.
Six weeks of wondrous country, sandy desert, billabongs,
campfire dinners, elders' legends, drovers' tales and songs.

Highjack, my horse, stamps and kicks, I'm worried he might roam.
He takes two days to settle down, make friends and feel at home.
We rise at five before first light and find our horses saddled,
the drovers call, the stock whips crack, the riders prepare to straddle.
The dust clouds up, the cattle groan, small calves are running by,
'Keep them close!' young Bridie shouts, 'but gently now,' she adds.

'We've over seven long miles to go, and mustn't let them lag.'
We'll stop for lunch at Dickeree, to holding yards they'll go,
and then the Simpson Desert dunes will guide the cattle flow.

Our horses love the desert sand, their hooves sink deep and soft,
but we need a strong hand to stop them rolling their riders off!
Four dingoes sit on sandy dunes and watch the mob move by,
they hope a calf might break away and save their search for supper.
A carcass lies on rocky ground with eagles circling high,
they soar and glide, then land astride, to feast upon their quarry.

Six days have passed, and we are all seduced by this famous track,
the colour, smells, rhythm of life, makes us part of the great outback.
The mob looks good, the drovers say, and the horses are now a herd,
as we hand our reins to riders new, and emotions falter words.
My bag is packed, the tent re-zipped, goodbyes are fond and true.
We drive to the pub, climb into the plane, and take off into the blue.

A Swedish Life

2010–2013, Alingsås

Alingsås, our new home in a small country town,
potatoes have been the reason for its renown.
Between lakes it lies, and a silvery stream
winds through the woodland, a Swedish dream.
Life within nature, hunter–gatherers seen
fishing for perch and picking wild flowers –
midsommar's light stays with us for hours.
Our small *radhus* is shrouded by trees,
woodpeckers tap, there's the hum of bees.
A walking trail leads to the lake's lower reaches,
where tons of white sand turns the bank into beaches
for family picnics, swimming and fun –
memories to store when wintertime comes.

Midsommar madness swings into gear,
summer solstice the essence of each passing year.
This old pagan rite to ensure fertility,
challenges each Swede, tests their ability
to gather wildflowers and twine into wreaths
and deck a maypole with fresh twigs and leaves.
Linking hands, young and old, with family and friends,
chant rhymes, sing songs and, with calls from the host,
charge their glasses and sing a series of toasts.

This longest of parties continues all night,
with the countryside basked in mellow dusk light.

Magnus joins us, a giant schnauzer puppy,
strong willed and mischievous, stubborn and naughty.
He has us entranced, but it's a challenge to train him,
long walks round the lake, a good way to calm him.
His name becomes known in this small country town,
his affectionate nature wins over the frowns.
He grows adult size in a flash and stands out
as a rebel, when well-behaved dogs are about.

Hijab-clad women, heads shrouded in black,
alert him to danger, he considers an attack.
He rounds them up barking, they shriek out in fright,
their hands wave about, their robes are askew,
I apologise, grab him and back well away
Red faced, and head home, away from the fray.
Appalled at his show of misbehaviour,
we focus our training on flowing regalia.

So it's puppy school for Magnus, language school for me,
Encouraged by Kerstin's Swedish family.
The course is attended by refugees
fleeing chaos and turmoil, despotic regimes,
in Kabul, Baghdad and Palestine.
We must speak only Swedish at lesson time!
Frustrated at first, I'm out of my depth,
but slowly I realise this method is best.

My new friends share stories of harrowing times –
wars, persecution, loved ones left behind.
Overcome with gratitude and smiling with pride,
their new country Sweden stands at their side.
Cold weather forgotten, this culture so strange,
they're safe here now and well out of range
of the bombs, there's a benefit right from the start,
they'll master the language, take customs to heart.

This church bell has tolled across the valley
since early AD at the Varnhem Abbey.
Cistercian monks at first maintained it,
Vikings used force to own and to claim it.
Now it's the Swedish Church's turn to retain it.
Cloister gardens in bloom, add colour to the gloom.
Honeysuckles climbing high, Viking graves nearby.

Today it's neatly ordered with a line of chairs,
a groomed lawn and font in the Abbey square.
Guests gather here and the family formally greets
members of Clergy before taking their seats.
The robed padre speaks, there are hymns and prayers,
for the Christening, birds twittering, the soft scent of flowers,
A bell chimes as it gently sways high in the tower.
A smorgasbord luncheon set up by the lake,
marks this day as special for Tilda Elle's sake.

Winter's first snow falls, a challenge to our travel,
iced lakes and snowdrifts, paths sprinkled with gravel,
spikes clipped to shoes, to stop us sliding on the ice.
Magnus bombs snow mounds, and rolls over twice.
We ferry the children on sledges called *pulkas.*
They squeal with delight as they slide on the snow,
with shopping bags balanced as homeward we go.

A sauna hut sits on the lake's foreshore.
It's fire stoked for hours to heat up the coals
to forty degrees. Water buckets infused
with eucalypts, herbs to pour and make steam,
the chimney puffs smoke, it works like a dream.
The ritual is strict, we enter and strip,
sit on towels and cook, like lambs on a spit.
When steam and heat causes rivers of sweat
we run from the hut, dive into the lake
or roll nude in the snow, scream and shout –
then return to the sauna for another bout.
At last, wrapped in towels, it's time to retire,
and retreat to relax by the family-room fire.

The Christmas calendar is hung with care,
each day in December has a window to share.
Instructions and prompting for Christmas fare –
there's marzipan cookies and *gloegg* to prepare,
gingerbread biscuits and cinnamon rolls,
candles lit everywhere, welcoming trolls.

The Christmas tree choice is a family affair,
we search the woods for a pine tree rare.
Each tree is discussed in a family forum,
its height and breadth, before one is chosen.
We line up and carry it home with a song –
decoration and toasts may go all night long.

Lucia begins on the twelfth of December.
Girls in white, wearing candlelit wreaths, parade
through the town. There's a band and carols are played.
They come to the square and the mayor has his say.
A party, hot doughnuts, mulled wine mark this day.
Christmas Eve we assemble with family and friends,
exchange gifts round the tree to shouts of delight,
with dinner to follow well into the night.
A walk through the snow on a winding path,
midnight mass in a chapel at the forest's heart.

These three years in Sweden bring insights, impressions
of the value of home life and ancient traditions.
Swedes enjoy their culture through simple pleasures –
by any means, a great philosophy to treasure.

radhus – town house; *midsommar* – mid summer; *gloegg* – mulled wine

Author's Note

This book is an attempt to showcase my love of language by telling stories in verse. These are vignettes describing events over the decades, snapshots of the human condition during different eras. My writing is often prompted by wars and disruption, but always features examples of the human spirit, and its capacity to survive and thrive.

I believe connection with the natural world of wildlife and wild habitats is the answer to a world that worships materialism and instant gratification. We owe it to future generations to pass on this message, and by doing so they will inherit a rich and rewarding future.

Heather Caddick, 2018

Wakefield Press is an independent publishing and distribution company based in Adelaide, South Australia. We love good stories and publish beautiful books. To see our full range of books, please visit our website at wakefieldpress.com.au where all titles are available for purchase. To keep up with our latest releases, news and events, subscribe to our monthly newsletter.

Find us!

Facebook: facebook.com/wakefield.press
Twitter: twitter.com/wakefieldpress
Instagram: instagram.com/wakefieldpress

Printed in Australia
AUOW01n1831180718
300318AU00001B/1

9 781743 055724